POPULAR CULTURE

A VIEW FROM THE PAPARAZZI

Orlando Bloom	John Legend
Kelly Clarkson	Lindsay Lohan
Johnny Depp	Mandy Moore
Hilary Duff	Ashlee and Jessica Simpson
Will Ferrell	
Jake Gyllenhaal	Justin Timberlake
Paris and Nicky Hilton	Owen and Luke Wilson
LeBron James	Tiger Woods

Paris and Nicky Hilton

Emma Carlson Berne

Mason Crest Publishers

Paris and Nicky Hilton

FRONTIS
The wealthy and fashionable sisters Paris and Nicky Hilton are among the most photographed young women on the planet.

Produced by 21st Century Publishing and Communications, Inc.

MASON CREST PUBLISHERS INC.
370 Reed Road
Broomall, Pennsylvania 19008
(866) MCP-BOOK (toll free)
www.masoncrest.com

Printed in the United States.

First Printing

9 8 7 6 5 4 3 2 1

Library of Congress Cataloging-in-Publication Data

Berne, Emma Carlson.
   Paris and Nicky Hilton / Emma Carlson Berne.
      p. cm.—(Pop culture : a view from the paparazzi)
   Includes bibliographical references and index.
   Hardback edition: ISBN-13: 978-1-4222-0204-3
   Paperback edition: ISBN-13: 978-1-4222-0358-3
 1. Hilton, Paris, 1981–   2. Hilton, Nicholai Olivia, 1983–   3. Celebrities—United States—Biography—Juvenile literature. 4. Socialites—United States—Biography—Juvenile literature. 5. Models (Persons)—United States—Biography—Juvenile literature. 6. Actors—United States—Biography—Juvenile literature. I. Title.
CT275.H59926B47 2008
973.93092'2—dc22   2007008990

Publisher's notes:
- All quotations in this book come from original sources, and contain the spelling and grammatical inconsistencies of the original text.

- The Web sites mentioned in this book were active at the time of publication. The publisher is not responsible for Web sites that have changed their addresses or discontinued operation since the date of publication. The publisher will review and update the Web site addresses each time the book is reprinted.

CONTENTS

Paris and Nicky Hilton always attract attention whenever they show up at a club opening or awards show. This photograph of the two socialites was taken as the Hilton sisters were preparing to walk into the 2003 MTV Video Music Awards show at Radio City Music Hall in New York City.

1

Two Successful Sisters

To their many adoring fans, Paris and Nicky Hilton seem like exotic superstars: tall and lean, incredibly wealthy, and always wearing fabulous outfits. Paris's signature smirk pouts from tabloid pages every week, while Nicky's sweet smile graces the runways of Milan and New York. But who are these wild and wealthy young women?

Paris and Nicky Hilton are not singers, actors, artists, or musicians. They are rich, but there are plenty of even wealthier people who are completely unknown to the general public. So why does practically every person in the United States know their names? Perhaps the main reason for their **notoriety** is that Paris and Nicky have interesting and glamorous lives. People are interested in what they are doing and wearing, so companies will pay a lot of money to have their pictures on magazine covers or their presence at club or restaurant openings. Paris and Nicky can always be expected to show up in stunning outfits, accompanied by an **entourage** of equally attractive friends.

Of course, Paris and Nicky had some help on their way to fame. Their great-grandfather Conrad Hilton started the Hilton hotel chain, and the girls are heiresses to part of his enormous fortune. Thanks to their family's wealth, the sisters have traveled in the circles of the American elite for their entire lives. They have lived in fancy New York apartments, as well as on a Bel-Air estate. When they were only teenagers, they made their debut as "celebutantes"—celebrity debutantes. That word was made up just to describe heiresses who have become famous for their wild lifestyles, just like the Hilton sisters.

The girls have been busy since their celebutante days. Today, neither is content just to shop all day and dance at clubs all night. Both Nicky and Paris have turned their beauty, sense of style, and dynamite personalities into fortunes of their own.

Living the *Simple Life*

In 2003, average Americans from Maine to California clicked on their televisions and were treated to the sight of beautiful, diamond-encrusted Paris Hilton crouching in an Arkansas barnyard, milking a cow along with her equally beautiful and wealthy friend Nicole Richie. Surprised viewers soon realized that they had tuned into a new reality show on the Fox network, *The Simple Life*. Paris was already something of a celebrity, but when *The Simple Life* turned out to be a hit it catapulted her to even greater fame. During the show Paris and Nicole lived with the Leding family on a farm outside of a tiny Arkansas town for five weeks. They had to rise early to milk cows and take care of the farm chores.

During the show the girls played up their image as pampered and sheltered rich brats. In one scene, when Nicole asked the Ledings if they shop at the discount retail store Wal-Mart, Paris innocently asked, "What's Wal-Mart?" Some viewers were shocked by how rude and spoiled the girls seemed. But Paris later explained that she was exaggerating parts of her **persona** to make the show funny. She later told Donna Freydkin of *USA Today*:

> **"I was playing a character. I'm totally normal. I think it's obnoxious when people demand limos or bodyguards. I eat at McDonald's or Taco Bell."**

Viewers did not care whether Paris was playing a role or showing her true self. By the end of the first season of *The Simple Life*, nearly 13 million people were tuning in for each episode. Fox renewed the show for two more seasons, filming the adventures of Nicole and Paris all over the country. After that, a fourth season of *The Simple Life* was produced for the E! cable channel.

Paris Hilton became a household name with the success of her 2003 reality television show *The Simple Life*. The show, which aired on the Fox network, featured Paris and her good friend Nicole Richie doing a variety of jobs while living on an Arkansas farm. The show was an immediate hit, drawing nearly 13 million viewers each week.

Unlike her older sister, who has appeared on television and in movies, Nicky Hilton has focused on a career in fashion and clothing design. In this photo she shows off one of her more than 300 handbags. Nicky has had an opportunity to design handbags for several highly respected firms, including the upscale Japanese company Samantha Thavasa.

One Hot Chick

Paris's younger sister Nicky has also promoted herself, but has kept a lower profile. Nicky has always been interested in fashion, and has designed handbags since she was 17. For a short time, Nicky even attended the Parsons School of Design and the Fashion Institute of Technology in Manhattan. In 2003, as Paris was becoming a household name, Nicky debuted her own line of clothing and accessories, called "Chick by Nicky Hilton."

Chick puts a feminine spin on ordinary clothes: pink chiffon hoodies, jeans with air-brushed angels, jeweled tank tops. "I like things that are sweet, like a jeweled cardigan with a pair of shorts," Hilton told Houston journalist Heather Staible. Nicky wanted the clothes to feel accessible to different types of girls. She said to Staible,

> **❝I have been asked 'Why didn't you charge $400 for a pair of jeans?' But I didn't want to do it that way. I wanted the line to be accessible to young girls. I think it's ridiculous that these young girls look in the magazines and feel they won't be socially accepted or cool if they don't have the $500 Prada bag or a pair of $700 Dolce & Gabbana jeans. I wanted [Chick to be] tasteful and sophisticated without the high prices.❞**

Chick clothes are carried at middle-range department stores like Dillards, but the handbags Nicky has designed are sold at expensive shops and trendy **boutiques**. Nicky loves handbags. She has told journalists that she has over 300—so many that she never carries the same handbag two days in a row.

Nicky and Paris both have proven to be successful entrepreneurs. They were given a boost at the start however, beginning with two doting and wealthy parents and the privileges that come with the Hilton name.

The Hilton family—Barron, Nicky, parents Kathy and Rick, Paris, and Conrad—pose with Mickey Mouse at Walt Disney World Resort in Florida during February 2005. The family was at the resort to celebrate Paris's birthday. Paris and Nicky are descended from the famous hotel chain founder Conrad Hilton, and will one day inherit a share of the Hilton fortune.

2

Growing Up Hilton

Even though they were born in New York City, Paris and Nicky have always been California girls. They grew up in the fashionable and exclusive community of Bel-Air in Los Angeles, where their parents, Rick and Kathy Hilton, owned a mansion. The Hiltons fit right in with their wealthy and powerful neighbors.

Rick Hilton, Paris and Nicky's father, is the grandson of Conrad Hilton, the businessman who started the world-famous Hilton hotel chain. Conrad was a smart man who believed in the philosophy of "work hard, play hard." He started renting out his family home in Texas as a hotel in the early 1900s. Within a few decades, he had built a hotel empire. Conrad had great fun along the way too: in 1942, he married sexy Hungarian actress Zsa Zsa Gabor. They had a wild, **tempestuous** relationship until their divorce in 1946.

Conrad had three sons: William (Rick Hilton's father), Eric, and Conrad Junior, whom everyone called Nick. Nick Hilton was a famous character in his own right: he was extremely handsome and had a reputation as a hard-partying playboy. In 1950 Nick Hilton married the young English actress Elizabeth Taylor, but their marriage lasted only about a year.

Rick and Kathy

Rick knew all about his uncle Nick's wild behavior, but he lived a more ordinary life—if being exceedingly wealthy can be called ordinary. Rick grew up in a giant house in Santa Monica, California. He had seven **siblings**, and was friendly with the children of many famous people. Rick was a sweet, shy boy who generally stayed out of trouble. However, while he was a student at the University of Denver Rick gained a reputation for throwing huge parties with bands and food in the ballroom of the Denver Hilton. During his last year at the university, Rick started dating a blonde girl he had known since high school named Kathy Richards.

Kathy had lived a very different sort of life than Rick Hilton. She grew up in Encino, California, where she lived with her mother and a series of stepfathers. Kathy's mother was a tough, driven woman who was determined that her daughter was going to be a big star. Kathy started modeling when she was two years old, and by the time she was 13 she had appeared in dozens of television commercials. She also took singing and dancing lessons, and learned how to play the guitar, ride horses, and swim, in hopes of furthering her show business career. Kathy did make a few appearances on several television shows such as *Happy Days* and *The Rockford Files* during the late 1970s. However, although she was beautiful and perky, her career never really took off.

Kathy was only 18 when she married Rick Hilton in a lavish Beverly Hills wedding. Fifteen months later, on February 17, 1981, their first daughter, Paris Whitney Hilton, was born.

A Young Family

The Hiltons set up residence in an expensive apartment in New York City. Baby Paris was christened at St. Patrick's Cathedral in Manhattan

Although Paris and Nicky's father, Rick Hilton, came from a wealthy family, he has worked hard to build his own fortune. Rick Hilton has earned millions from his successful real-estate development company. In 1978 he married Kathy Richards, an aspiring actress. She gave birth to Paris in 1981 and Nicky in 1983.

and everyone who saw her remarked on her extraordinary beauty. She had a perfect doll face and corn silk blond hair. Paris grew even more lovely as she grew older. Kathy treated her like a little doll. When Paris was only a toddler Kathy styled her hair, painted her face with mascara and eyeshadow, and called her "Star."

On October 5, 1983, Rick and Kathy's second daughter, Nicholai Olivia Hilton, was born in New York. Everyone called her "Nicky" after her famous uncle Nick, but sometimes they also called her "Chick" because of her fluffy blond hair.

By the mid-1980s, Rick and Kathy were ready for a change from apartment living and the cold weather of New York. They moved the family back to California, and bought a house in Bel-Air. Paris and Nicky remember their childhood as a happy one. Kathy was a young mother who had a lot of energy to lavish on her pretty blonde daughters. Rick was a kind and doting father who always found time for his children even while he was building his own fortune as a successful real estate developer. In her autobiography *Confessions of an Heiress*, Paris wrote:

> **"My dad . . . was the support system in the house. . . . He got us through every crisis. . . . Even though I'm the oldest, I admit, I *am* still daddy's little girl."**

Memories of Childhood

The Hiltons were a large, close-knit family. Kathy and Rick had two more children (both boys) by the mid-1990s. Barron was born in 1990 and Conrad in 1994. All of Rick's seven siblings also had their own children, so Paris and Nicky had a lot of cousins to play with when they were growing up. The girls also played with their mother's younger sisters, Kyle and Kim Richards, who had both been well-known child actresses when they were younger. Paris remembers the whole family coming over for lavish Easter-egg hunts and Christmas parties.

Animals were a big part of the girls' lives. Kathy and Rick would buy them chicks and baby rabbits every Easter. When she was twelve, Paris had a pet ferret she called Farrah the Ferret. Farrah would ride around in Paris's purse.

Of course, the girls did not spend all their time playing. They both attended a Catholic school, St. Paul the Apostle. The teachers and principal were very strict, and would not even let the students have boy-girl dances until their eighth-grade graduation. After Paris completed her

Paris wrote about her childhood experiences in her 2004 memoir *Confessions of an Heiress*. She also provided advice to those who wanted to emulate her lifestyle: "If you can channel your own inner heiress . . . and project an extreme sense of confidence—even if you don't really feel it every moment— people will treat you differently."

The Hilton sisters always had pets when they were growing up. When she was 12 years old, Paris owned a pet ferret, which she would carry around in her purse. As an adult Paris still likes exotic pets, and currently owns a kinkajou (a ferret-like rainforest mammal) named Baby Luv and a Chihuahua named Tinkerbell.

education at St. Paul's in 1995, she attended Marymount High School for a year. After that, in 1996 the family moved back to New York City. Some members of the Hilton family thought that the family moved because Kathy wanted her daughters to experience society life in New York.

Big City Life

After returning to New York, the Hiltons lived in the penthouse of the Waldorf Towers, a residential section of the Waldorf-Astoria Hotel, which is owned by the Hilton Hotels Corporation. By this time 15-year-old Paris and 12-year-old Nicky were starting to attract attention in the social scene. Both girls were blonde, beautiful, and chic. Nicky was enrolled at the all-girls Catholic school Convent of the Sacred Heart, but Paris told her mother she didn't want to go to a girls' school. She persuaded her parents to send her to the Professional Children's School, a school for young actors, dancers, and musicians.

Paris and Nicky later told Nancy Jo Sales of *Vanity Fair* magazine that when they moved from Bel-Air, they thought they would hate New York. Nicky said,

> **"I cried.... Everything was, like, different. Like when I was in L.A. in seventh grade we would just all sit home on Friday night and watch movies and like, make up dances, and in New York there's, like, house parties and boys."**

Soon though, the girls realized that there was much to like about New York. They hung out with their friends from Los Angeles, along with some new friends: Nicole Richie, the daughter of pop star Lionel Richie; Kidada Jones, whose father was music producer Quincy Jones; and Bijou Phillips, daughter of John Philips of the 1960s music group The Mamas and the Papas. The girls would wear crazy clothes and makeup and then go out to clubs and parties. Even though they were all still in their teens, the girls managed to get into the clubs, where they would dance and party all night.

Getting Noticed

Nicky was doing well in her studies at Sacred Heart but Paris was another story. Even though she was smart, she was not interested in school. What's more, she was not happy at the Professional Children's

Nicky Hilton hangs out with Nicole Richie at a party. Although the Hilton sisters did not want to move from Los Angeles to New York, they soon made many new friends among the wealthy young people living in the city. Both Paris and Nicky soon gained a reputation for spending their nights at wild parties with other glamorous people.

School. She liked the other kids she met, like Christina Ricci and Macauley Culkin, but unlike most of the students Paris was not really interested in an acting career. She preferred to party. In her junior year, Paris left PCS and enrolled in the Dwight School, an exclusive prep school in a fancy New York neighborhood.

Outside of the New York club circles in which they moved, few people had ever heard of Nicky and Paris Hilton. That began to change in 1999, when Nicky was 15 and Paris was 18. That year, a reporter for the *New York Times* Style section attended a "Sweet 16" party for Marissa Bregman, the daughter of a Hollywood movie producer. The party was held in the ballroom of the River Club, a famous private club, and featured hordes of wealthy young New Yorkers drinking champagne and dancing to hip-hop music.

The reporter was especially interested in young Nicky Hilton. Nicky, she later wrote, had everyone in the room staring at her when she and her friend Olympia Scarry started grabbing boys at random from the dance floor and kissing them while dancing. But this was nothing new for the teenager, the reporter wrote:

> **"Olympia and Nicky both can pass for much older, and say they have little trouble getting into clubs or being served alcohol. In fact, they are familiar enough with the night scene as 10th graders to be a little jaded, and prefer . . . private Sweet 16 parties [like Bregman's] instead."**

Wild Times for Paris

Paris was having her own fun. Sometime during her senior year at Dwight, she disappeared from view. The details of this incident are not clear. Kathy Hilton later told the media that a stalker was bothering Paris, and that the family had to hide at the London Hilton, taking a tutor with them. However, in his book *House of Hilton*, journalist Jerry Oppenheimer wrote that it was rumored at the time that Paris had run away with a trucker who was unloading goods at the Waldorf. No one knows what the real story is—all that is known for certain is that around this time Paris's parents sent her to live with her grandmother, Kathy's mother, in Rancho Mirage, California.

Paris' grandmother, Kathy Richards, enrolled her at the exclusive Palm Valley School in Rancho Mirage. Paris didn't like this school any better than she had liked Dwight, but at least she had a jeweled calculator to help her through algebra classes. Paris eventually earned her high school degree in 2000.

Paris later said she enjoyed living with her grandmother. Kathy Richards was a formidable woman who had controlled her own daughter's life completely, and she knew that her granddaughter was destined for fame. She did everything she could to increase Paris's media exposure. When *Vanity Fair* magazine called, looking to do a story on the Hilton sisters, Kathy Richards offered her own Beverly Hills condo for the photo shoot. In September 2000 the magazine featured photos of Paris lying on a couch in her grandmother's living room, wearing a mesh thong.

"Setting Society on Its Ear"

The *Vanity Fair* story was the first major media exposure centered exclusively around the Hilton sisters. Journalist Nancy Jo Sales wrote in her introduction to the piece:

Paris, then 19 years old, poses for a photograph to accompany a magazine article. By early 2001 numerous stories had been written about the Hilton sisters. Paris and Nicky became targets of the paparazzi—freelance photographers who follow famous people around hoping to get shocking or scandalous snapshots they can sell to magazines or tabloid newspapers.

❝[A] fourth Hilton generation—19-year-old Paris, with her 16-year-old sister, Nicky, in her wake—is setting society on its ear. . . . Paris is the very model of a hip-hop debutante.❞

Celebrity watchers were fascinated. These two girls fulfilled every American's dream of pure fame: they were beautiful, cool, shocking, and always living what seemed to be a fabulous life of parties and shopping. They hung out with other socialites, like Casey Johnson, heiress to the Johnson & Johnson pharmaceutical fortune, and Amanda Hearst, who will one day inherit a chunk of the Hearst Publishing empire. Paris was seen with several young men, including actors Edward Furlong and Leonardo DiCaprio, boxer Oscar De La Hoya, and musician Deryck Whibley of the band Sum 41. Nicky started dating Brian McFayden, who starred on several MTV programs. In 2001, Tom Rhodes of the *London Times* wrote that the Hiltons were:

❝[fixtures] at VIP rooms in nightclubs across the country. . . seen wearing the shortest skirts and fishnet stockings, partying until the early hours and showing scant regard for the media's chronicling of their every embarrassing moment.❞

But both Nicky and Paris were still young. They were used to wealth, but they were not used to fame. They would have stunning successes in the upcoming years, but they would have to get through some hard times first.

Paris and Nicky Hilton are pictured here attending the 2001 VH1/Vogue Fashion Awards in New York. The Hilton sisters have a very close relationship, and have always been the best of friends. When scandals occurred because of controversial behavior by either Paris or Nicky, their close friendship would help the sisters remain grounded.

3

Tough Times

Since they first appeared in the public eye, Paris and Nicky have always said that they are each other's best friends. Magazines are filled with photos of the two sisters leaning into each other and smiling, while wearing matching outfits. They have supported each other through every stage of their lives, no matter how difficult.

Paris has said that no one in the world understands her like her sister. She devotes an entire section of her memoir *Confessions of an Heiress* to Nicky, writing:

> **"The only person in the world who really knows me is Nicky. We'll always be there for each other. She's always proud of me, in the**

good times and the rough. And that's a wonderful thing to know and to have grown up with.

It is a good thing the sisters are so close. When problems arose, they would need each other's support more than ever.

Beginning Their Careers

After finishing high school, Paris took acting lessons and began pursuing a modeling career. She appeared in advertisements for designers like Tommy Hilfiger, Catherine Malandrino, and Marc Bouwer, and was pictured in magazines like *GQ*, *Vanity Fair*, and *People*. She even made a brief appearance in the Ben Stiller movie *Zoolander* (2001), which made fun of the modeling industry. Paris remained in the news by attending the hottest parties in New York and Los Angeles, and tabloid photographers began to follow her wherever she went.

Nicky, who graduated from Convent of the Sacred Heart high school in New York in 2001, was also drawing public attention for her partying lifestyle. The tabloids often photographed her out on the town, generally with a good-looking date. Two of her boyfriends at this time were the models Marcus Schenkenberg and Mark Vanderloo. But like Paris, Nicky was not content to spend all of her time partying She began studying fashion at the Parsons School of Design.

The growing public interest in the Hilton sisters led executives from the Fox television network to ask them to star in a reality TV show. Nicky preferred to avoid the limelight, and said she was not interested, but Paris accepted the Fox offer. In May 2003 she began taping *The Simple Life* with her good friend Nicole Richie.

Best of all, both sisters had found love. Nicky started dating a wealthy money manager named Todd Meister. Although 33-year-old Todd was 12 years older than 21-year-old Nicky, they had known each other for many years and she was crazy about him. Paris was just as happy. In 2002 she became engaged to Jason Shaw, a male model who had appeared in ads for Tommy Hilfiger's underwear line. Paris felt like she was finally settling down with a man she loved.

A Scandal Hits

Paris had no idea that her happy world was about to be shaken. Just before the first episode of *The Simple Life* was set to be aired on Fox, she learned that video clips showing her having sex with a former

After graduating from Convent of the Sacred Heart High School in 2001, Nicky took the first steps toward a career in fashion by enrolling in the Parsons School for Design in the Greenwich Village neighborhood of New York City. The school is highly regarded, with a faculty that includes some of the country's most talented fashion designers and artists.

boyfriend named Rick Salomon had been posted on the Internet. All of a sudden, everyone seemed to know about the embarrassing video. Paris told Austin Scaggs of *Rolling Stone* that after hearing about the tape,

"I was freaking out. I couldn't believe it. I was like 'there's no way, there's no way.' Then someone I knew told me that they'd seen it. I started crying."

When she heard about the tape, Paris immediately flew back to Los Angeles, feeling completely humiliated. She **sequestered** herself with her family in the Hamptons that for Thanksgiving, telling a reporter from USA Today:

Paris is photographed with boyfriend Rick Salomon outside a club in Southhampton, New York, in May 2001. In 2003, just before the premiere of *The Simple Life*, Paris was embarrassed when intimate video clips showing her with Salomon were posted on the Internet. She sued Salomon for releasing the tape, but the case was settled out of court in 2005.

❝I can't walk the streets. It's too embarrassing. I don't want to go out anymore. I don't want to party.❞

Dealing With Crisis

Rick and Kathy Hilton did their best to defuse the scandal. They hired a public relations consultant to advise Paris on what she needed to do, and both parents made public statements of unconditional love and support. Rick Hilton told the *New York Daily News*:

> **❝I love my daughter more than anything in the whole world. It goes without saying that I was severely unhappy knowing that such a tape exists. But I support her in every way humanly possible.❞**

Soon, the public learned the story behind the scandal. Paris had begun dating Rick Salomon in 2000, when she was only 19. At one point in their relationship, they had made a videotape of themselves partying and having sex. The tape was supposed to

Some people speculated that Paris had engineered the release of the explicit video herself in order to generate publicity that would help *The Simple Life* become a hit. Paris strongly denied this rumor, telling *GQ* magazine in 2006, "I never received a dime from it. [Salomon] should give [the money] to some charity for the sexually abused or something."

be private, but three years later someone sold it to a Seattle-based company that produced **pornographic** videos. The seller's name has never been revealed, although some people have speculated that it was a former roommate of Salomon, or that it might have been Salomon himself.

A few people even speculated that Paris herself had somehow engineered the release of the tape to coincide with the premiere of *The Simple Life*. After all, the publicity from the scandal increased Paris's name recognition. Kimberly Strassal of the *Wall Street Journal* wrote that with the appearance of the tape,

> **"[suddenly] the girl who by last year already was 'overexposed' landed back on top of the news. . . . You have to wonder if the one person having a really good laugh over the uproar is Paris herself."**

Making Changes

According to Paris, however, the last thing she ever wanted was this sort of scandal. She told Austin Scaggs of *Rolling Stone*:

> **"I thought my whole life was over. . . . I was so embarrassed. I could not believe someone I loved could do that to me."**

Paris decided she needed some changes in her life. In December 2003, she ended her engagement to Jason Shaw. Soon she began dating Nick Carter, a young singer with a wholesome image who was a member of the popular band Backstreet Boys. She spent more time with her sister Nicky and her parents. She also began thinking more about her future career choices, ultimately deciding that she should become more serious about acting and singing.

Paris's embarrassment was eased by the success of *The Simple Life*, which first aired on December 2, 2003. The show was a surprise hit, as more than 10 million people tuned in for the first episode and the audience grew for subsequent shows. People seemed to enjoy the antics of Paris and Nicole Richie, who had left their cell phones and credit cards at home and were living on a small farm in Arkansas. The two rich girls tried many jobs—including plucking chickens, milking cows, and working at a fast-food restaurant—but ended up

Paris appears with Nick Carter, singer for the Backstreet Boys, at a charity event in 2004. She started dating the pop star after breaking up with Jason Shaw. Carter was so smitten with the heiress that he had "Paris" tattooed on his wrist. However, in July 2004 the relationship ended.

getting fired from all of them. Dana Walden, the president of the Fox Television network, said:

> **❝It's just fantastic TV. It's funny, it's charming. You felt that these women were genuinely in an environment that was so foreign to them and yet they were trying their best.❞**

The program was so successful that Fox quickly released the first seven episodes on DVD, and also created some new episodes to cash in on the show's popularity. The network's executives quickly signed Paris and Nicole up for a second season.

Hard Lessons Learned

The sex-tape scandal and *The Simple Life* made Paris even more famous than she had been before. For better or for worse, the heiress admitted, the scandal surrounding the intimate video had certainly changed her life. "After that experience, I learned that you just have to laugh at yourself," Paris told Scaggs. "It was a bad thing that happened, and I learned so much from it. My life is better now."

Paris later said that she thought that going through the horror of having the tape distributed helped her grow up. In her book *Confessions of an Heiress*, she wrote:

> **❝I've done some pretty immature things [in my life], but this is the fate of every heiress. Everyone does crazy stuff when they're young . . . and everything tends to get written about so people don't forget as easily. I learned this lesson the hard way. Now I know that everyone's had embarrassing moments but we don't really hear about them if they're not famous.❞**

Through the scandal, Nicky was right there beside Paris, as she always had been. But in 2004 it was Nicky's turn to generate publicity with some crazy antics of her own.

A Surprise Wedding

In August 2004, Nicky and Paris boarded a chartered flight to Las Vegas for a weekend of fun. The sisters brought along a few of their friends,

Although the sex-tape scandal made Paris more famous than she had ever been before, it was not the kind of attention that she wanted. She later spoke a great deal about the way that the difficult and embarrassing experience had changed her life. "I learned so much from it," she said. "My life is better now."

In August 2004 it was Nicky Hilton's turn in the media spotlight, when she suddenly married her boyfriend Todd Meister in Las Vegas. Nicky later told *Women's Wear Daily* that she was surprised by the attention, saying, "I didn't know it would be such a big deal. We've been best friends forever." The marriage only lasted three months.

including actress Tara Reid, Nicole Richie, Rod Stewart's daughter Kimberly Stewart, and Bijou Phillips. The group started drinking and partying on the flight to Vegas. The partying continued after everyone checked into the ritzy Palms hotel and casino.

On Saturday, August 14, Todd Meister flew in on a private jet to join the group. The partying got even wilder. At 2:30 on Sunday morning everyone piled into cars and drove to the Clark County courthouse, where Nicky and Todd applied for a marriage license. Paris, Bijou, Nicky, and Todd then headed next door to the Vegas Wedding Chapel. Paris walked her sister down the aisle to Whitney Houston's "I Will Always Love You." Todd gave Nicky a diamond ring that was estimated to be between nine and twelve carats and worth over a million dollars.

No one else from the family was present at the wedding, but a publicist for the couple insisted that it was a planned event. Paris though, indicated otherwise when she later told *Rolling Stone* that "everyone was like 'Do it! Do it!' It was stupid. We didn't think about it." Nonetheless, Nicky and Todd were very much in love, friends told the media. One friend of Todd's told *People* magazine:

> **"[This] is a perfect place to start. They are both young, attractive, sophisticated. They might have a real chance."**

The Break-Up

The sentiment was hopeful but unfortunately did not prove true. Three months later, the newlyweds were granted an **annulment**. It wasn't the right time for Nicky to be a wife, she decided. She wanted to focus on her career and being Mrs. Todd Meister just didn't factor into that equation.

The split was **amicable**, however. After the annulment was finalized, the couple issued a statement that read:

> **"Both parties have ended the marriage amicably and they remain good friends."**

The incident did tarnish Nicky's reputation as the more sensible, level-headed Hilton sister, however—especially since Nicky was trying to be taken more seriously as a fashion designer. But as with Paris's sex tape scandal, after the surprise short-lived wedding the world knew the name "Nicky Hilton" just a little better.

Paris and Nicky Hilton ride the Big Thunder Mountain roller coaster at Disney World in Florida together. In many ways, over the past several years the lives of the Hilton sisters have been like roller-coaster rides. Both have experienced many ups and downs, but throughout all of the turmoil their lives have been exciting.

4

Rise to the Top

Scandals aside, the rise to fame of Paris and Nicky Hilton has been bumpy in other ways. Many people have wondered publicly *why* the girls are so famous—why there are paparazzi cameras waiting to photograph them at every club and restaurant they visit, and why tabloids are filled with stories and photos of their every move?

Some people complain that Paris and Nicky's fame is not appropriate, as they have not made great contributions to literature, theater, film, music, or any other cultural body of work, but are famous primarily just for being famous. Paris, the higher-profile sister, has attracted more critics. In his biography of the Hilton family, author Jerry Oppenheimer explained:

> **"Paris had become one of those celebrities many people loved to hate; her fame and infamy had provoked schadenfreude around the world. If anyone understood the shallowness of celebrity culture in the early years of the twenty-first century, it was the Hilton gal."**

There has been a backlash against the Hilton sisters. One famous New York gossip critic was so irritated by what he considered Paris's desire for attention that he declared that he would no longer mention her exploits in his newspaper column. The owner of a new bar in Manhattan told *USA Today* that he had denied Paris and her friends entrance, saying:

> **"I don't have anything personal against her. But I want a really sophisticated bar that's not part of that scene . . . [people] are really fed up with kowtowing to celebrities . . . making fools of themselves."**

But many people have also been supportive, and that has contributed to the girls' great success.

A Young Fashionista

After her highly publicized marriage, Nicky kept her sights focused on fashion and the modeling industry. During New York Fashion Week in fall 2004, she walked the runway in Croatian designer Raika D's show. She was a huge success. The newsletter *Fashion Windows* reported,

> **"When the spotlights came on, Nicky Hilton was the first model on the runway. . . . With shades of blue and black, lace and other rhinestone details, the young heiress looked innocent and sweet. . . . Closing the show, Nicky Hilton wore an iridescent blue embroidered taffeta fishtail gown making her look like exactly who and what she is—a young debutante ready to enter society."**

Paris is photographed outside the Ed Sullivan Theatre in New York after arriving for an appearance on the *Late Show with David Letterman*, June 2006. Although her work as an entertainer includes several successful seasons of *The Simple Life* and appearances in movies like *House of Wax*, Paris remains famous primarily for being a wealthy and beautiful socialite.

Nicky promotes her clothing line, Chick by Nicky Hilton, at a Macy's department store in New York City, March 2005. The clothes, intended for juniors and moderately priced, have been praised by fashion critics. Nicky has taken her career as a fashion designer very seriously, and in 2006 she released a second clothing line, Nicky Hilton Beverly Hills.

In December 2004 Nicky made an even grander entrance, when she and her business partners, Allen and Ross Fredman of Benvin Industries, rented an enormous office and showroom in the Fashion Center Building in downtown Manhattan. The store was meant to showcase her new fashion line, Chick by Nicky Hilton, which had just rolled out its first line of clothing designed by Nicky a few months earlier.

In an interview with *Women's Wear Daily*, Nicky explained how seriously she was taking the new business:

> **"[There are] so many celebrities who [just] lend their name to a line, which so takes all the fun out of it. I'm really hands-on. This [clothing line] is like a really big deal to me. I really want to put all my heart and soul in it."**

While she was enjoying the challenge of designing tank tops and other clothes, Nicky also appreciated the opportunity to create a line of purses for the Japanese handbag company Samantha Thavasa. Her modeling career seemed to be taking off as well, with her face appearing on many magazines around the world. In 2005 she and friend Kimberly Stewart were hired to represent the hip Australian underwear company Antz Pantz. A spokeswoman for the company explained why the two socialites were a good fit for the brand:

> **"Kimberly and Nicky really live with the Antz Pantz attitude and energy. They're pretty much the full-time party girls around town and Antz Pantz girls can really connect with that."**

Despite the busy schedule, Nicky also found a new love to spend time with: actor Kevin Connolly of the hit HBO series *Entourage*. They had dated briefly before Nicky married Todd, and resumed their relationship after the marriage ended. The couple portrayed themselves as downright boring, particularly compared to the craziness of the Meister affair. In July 2005 Kevin told *People* magazine:

> **"People would be disappointed in the normalcy of our relationship. We watch *Desperate Housewives* and fall asleep."**

Actress and Author

For Paris, the success of *The Simple Life* vaulted her to the peak of celebrity fame. Fox picked up the series for a second season in June 2004, allowing Paris and Nicole to continue their antics. This time they were filmed making a cross-country trip in a pink camper. The two made an entertaining duo: Nicole was a spitfire who shocked everyone with her **audacity**, while Paris seemed sweet but empty-headed. The girls were given no money for their trip, so they had to beg for it and work for people along the way in order to get food and gas. They took a number of unusual jobs, including plucking chickens (again) and working as maids at a nudist colony. Once again, the show was a huge hit.

Paris also became an author in 2004 with the publication of her memoir *Confessions of an Heiress*. The book combines stories about Paris's childhood and family experiences with general advice about how to live a fabulous life. *Publisher's Weekly* and *Hilary* magazine called the book "empowering" for young women, and it landed on the *New York Times* bestseller list.

The book features special tips on how to "act like an heiress." For example, Paris advised her readers, "Always tell everyone what they want to hear. Then do what you want. That way, no one ever gets mad at you. They get very confused and blame it on themselves." Also, in order to be like a true heiress, she suggested:

> **"Never wear the same thing twice. This is particularly important if you're going to be photographed a lot... If you double up, people will think you only have only one outfit—and that's annoying. And untrue."**

The next year Paris had her first real film acting role, with a small part in the horror movie *House of Wax*. (In *Zoolander* she had played herself.) The movie, which premiered in May 2005, starred Elisha Cuthbert and Chad Michael Murray. Paris's character Paige is a sexy blonde. However, she does not appear on screen very long before being murdered by a serial killer. *New York Times* film critic A.O. Scott wrote:

> **"[The movie] goes pretty much according to formula [with] the usual scary stuff—the sudden noises on the soundtrack, the shock cuts and camera tricks that never seem to grow old."**

Nicole Richie is seated while Paris holds a gas can in this promotional poster from the second season of *The Simple Life*. Subtitled *Road Trip*, the Fox series depicted the adventures of the two young women as they traveled across the United States. Paris drove their pink pickup truck, which hauled a trailer where the two socialites lived.

Although not everyone was impressed with Paris's short performance, she did win a 2005 Teen Choice Award for the Best Movie Scream Scene, and she was nominated for another Teen Choice Award for Breakout Performance by a female actor. She was also nominated for a 2006 MTV Movie Award for Best Frightened Performance. Paris herself was happy with the way the film turned out, telling film critic Rebecca Murray:

Paris and costar Robert Richard appear in a scene from the 2005 film *House of Wax*. Although many critics were hard on the film, *House of Wax* did earn over $68 million at the box office and another $42 million in DVD rentals. Although Paris was not onscreen for long, she won a Teen Choice Award for her performance.

> **"[House of Wax is] so scary and so good. . . . This one is creepy and scary and sexy and fun. It's a fun movie to go watch and scream and have a good time watching."**

Business Moves

During this time, Paris started becoming involved in other business ventures. In 2004 Parlux Fragrances released Paris's perfume, which was called simply "Paris Hilton." The next year Paris's second fragrance, "Just Me," was introduced. Paris would eventually create other perfumes, as well as a cologne for men.

Paris also licensed the use of her name to a nightclub in Orlando, Florida, which opened on December 30, 2004. Paris was paid more than a million dollars for her involvement with the nightclub, Club Paris. Although she helped to design the interior of the club (among her touches were pink couches and carpets, because pink is her favorite color), the main reason Paris was paid so much was that the owner knew her incredible popularity would attract other people to the nightclub. If Club Paris took off, he planned to open other clubs with her name in places like Las Vegas and New York.

As part of the deal, Paris was required to make regular appearances at Club Paris. Unfortunately, she was late for the opening of her club—she missed a flight from the Swiss Alps, where she had been on a skiing holiday. Her sister Nicky filled in for the ribbon-cutting that officially launched Club Paris.

Paris received other offers to make appearances at parties, for which she was usually paid fees of around $200,000. According to author Jerry Oppenheimer, Paris once made a million dollars for appearing at an event in Vienna. The fees added up to a nice annual income: *Business Week* estimated that Paris's 2005 income was more than $15 million.

Her success was more than just luck or her family's fortune.

> **"I always wanted to build a brand. Barbie's a brand. I knew I could be like that—an American princess,"**

she told Nancy Mills of the *New York Daily News*. Paris continued:

"Because of my last name, people think I'm spoiled. But I'm really down to earth, and I work harder than most people I know. I get up at 6 A.M., have meetings or photo shoots. Or I'm on the phone talking business or traveling to Tokyo to sell my perfume."

A Busy Personal Life

Not everything was perfect in Paris's life. In February 2005, someone hacked into her wireless phone account, downloaded her text messages and photos, and posted them on the Internet. Soon the 500 people in Paris's address book—including singers Ashlee Simpson and Avril Lavigne, actor Luke Wilson, tennis star Andy Roddick, and rapper Lil John—began receiving annoying emails and crank phone calls. "I got 2,000 emails in one day," Nicky later complained. The problem forced many of the celebrities to change their phone numbers.

In April Paris traveled to Las Vegas to model in a fashion show, wearing clothing designed by her sister. Soon after this, she admitted that she was no longer speaking to Nicole Richie, who had been one of her closest friends since they were children. Neither Nicole nor Paris ever explained why the two were no longer friends, but both refused to be filmed together for the fourth season of *The Simple Life*. The producers had to tape the girls doing separate activities with different families so they wouldn't even have to work together. Fox decided to cancel the show, although it was eventually picked up by the E! cable network.

Paris had some good things going on in her personal life as well. In May 2005, she announced that she was engaged to the young **scion** of a wealthy Greek shipping family, Paris Latsis. The couple had been dating for eight months. Paris told *People* magazine:

"I'm very in love—he's the one. . . . I want to have kids in the next two years, because I know that completes your life."

Just three months later, however, the two Parises announced that they were breaking up. Whatever the reason, Paris had decided that it

Paris appears on MTV's *Total Request Live* in July 2006; with her at the MTV Studio in Times Square, New York, is MTV VJ Damien Fahey. The heiress has kept herself in the public spotlight through appearances on programs like this one, understanding that good publicity will help her career as an entertainer to take off.

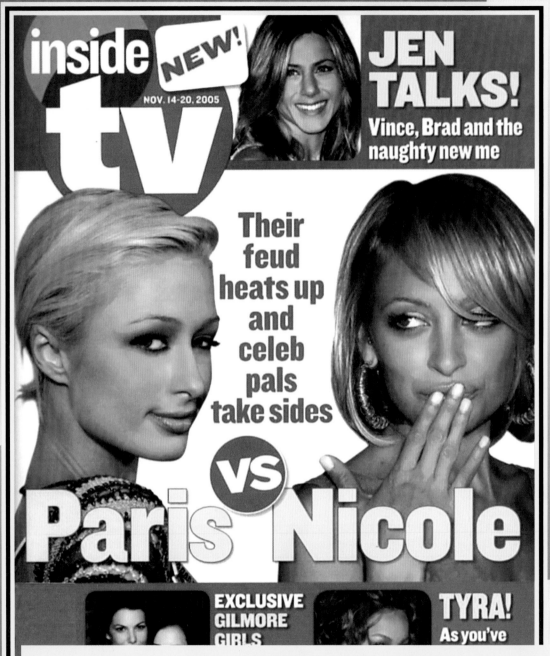

The split between Paris and Nicole Richie made the covers of many magazines. The two have never explained why they stopped speaking to each other. The friendship resumed after Paris called Nicole on her birthday in September 2006. "I really missed her and I just decided to pick up the phone and call her," Paris explained.

was not the right time to be married. In a statement, she explained:

> **"I just feel I'm not ready for marriage. I have seen the breakups between people who love each other and rush into getting married too quickly—and I do not want to make that mistake."**

Paris didn't let the breakup dampen her spirits though. Within weeks, she had found a new Greek boyfriend, Stavros Niarchos, who was also the heir to a shipping fortune. Soon, she and Stavros were photographed in every hot venue in Los Angeles and New York, kissing in booths and dancing in clubs.

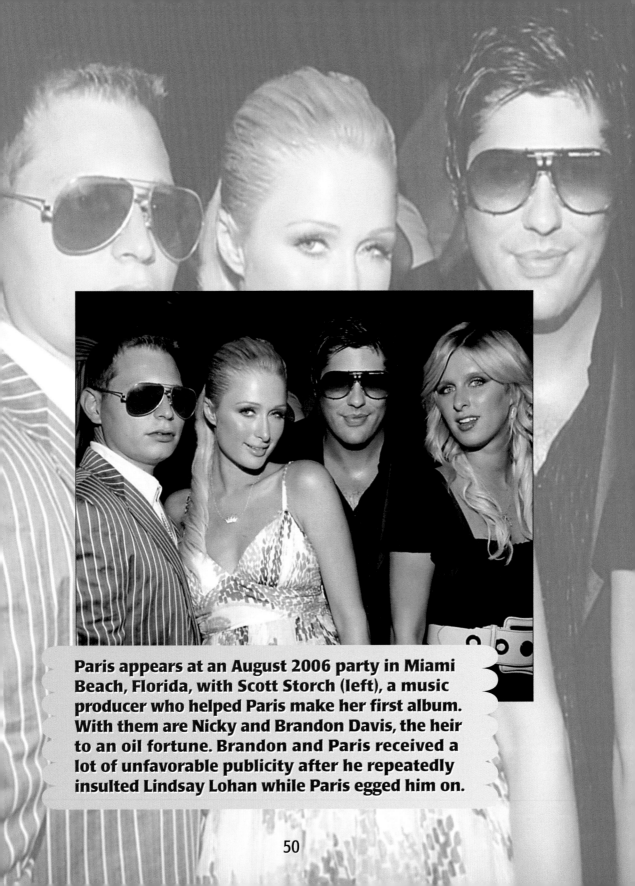

Paris appears at an August 2006 party in Miami Beach, Florida, with Scott Storch (left), a music producer who helped Paris make her first album. With them are Nicky and Brandon Davis, the heir to an oil fortune. Brandon and Paris received a lot of unfavorable publicity after he repeatedly insulted Lindsay Lohan while Paris egged him on.

5

Fabulous Lives

As the Hilton sisters have grown older, both have focused on expanding their careers into new areas. But even though they may not appear together at events or clubs wearing matching outfits and draped in expensive jewelry, as they once liked to do, Paris and Nicky are just as close as ever.

World by a String

Paris was there in February 2006 to support Nicky as she unveiled a new fashion line called Nicky Hilton Beverly Hills. Whereas the Chick line was aimed at girls and young teens, Nicky says that this new line includes clothes she and her friends would wear: sexy outfits inspired by rock 'n' roll music. When she was interviewed during the debut show for the line, Nicky made it clear that she is not just a celebrity designer. She told the Associated Press:

❝I don't want to be one of those celebrities that slaps their name on a label and collects royalty checks. Everything on that runway reflects me.❞

Also in 2006, Nicky had an opportunity to follow in her great-grandfather's footsteps. She signed an agreement to license her name to a hotel in South Beach, Florida, to be called Nicky O, a Nicky Hilton Hotel. (The O is for Olivia, Nicky's middle name.) Nicky was also asked to help design the interior of the 95-room hotel. However, by early 2007 the venture seemed to have hit some trouble, as construction fell behind schedule and its opening was delayed several times.

Singing Star

Paris has been focusing her attention on a new career: music. In 2006 she hooked up with celebrity music producer Scott Storch to make an album. Storch, who has produced songs for such stars as Beyonce, 50 Cent, and Justin Timberlake, told *Rolling Stone* that Paris had a voice like the 1980s rockers Cyndi Lauper or Debbie Harry. The two worked on nine songs for Paris's album and wound up dating at the same time. They released her first single, "Stars Are Blind," in June 2006. To the surprise of many critics, the song was a hit, reaching number 18 on the Billboard Hot 100 chart in the United States and doing even better among international audiences. It had a "fresh, sun-splashed reggae vibe," Chuck Taylor wrote in *Billboard*. "Sounds like Miss Paris could teach Top 40 superstars a thing or two about melody."

Her full-length album, titled *Paris*, was released in August 2006. Again, reviewers seemed pleasantly surprised. Keith Caulfield of *Billboard* called the record "an enjoyable pop romp," and wrote:

❝Does it matter that Paris Hilton isn't a great singer? Not really. [This album] won't change the world, but it's good fun.❞

In another review, the *All Music Guide* said Paris's debut album is "more fun than anything released by Britney Spears or Jessica Simpson, and a lot fresher, too."

In 2006 Warner Brothers collaborated with Nicky on a new collection of upscale licensed material. Called Tweety Designed by Nicky Hilton, the collection included stationery, personal care items, and materials for home decorating and pet grooming. In this promotional photo, Nicky is wearing Tweety jewelry, holding a Tweety handbag, and sitting on a Tweety-branded motorcycle.

Paris has said she is determined to make a career out of music. In *Confessions of an Heiress*, she wrote:

> **❝I'm going to keep . . . writing music, and hopefully I'll be able to follow this album with another. I'm quite serious about this music thing. I love it. . . . I barely have time to get into trouble anymore.❞**

Music has not stopped Paris from other business projects. In December 2006 she put out a new perfume, called Heiress. That same month, her film *National Lampoon's Pledge This!* was released on DVD. Unfortunately, the movie was not well received by critics. "Even by the low standards of the college comedy genre it's exceptionally awful," wrote James Sanford. Paris herself was not happy with the movie, because the producers had added some scenes that she did not like. She refused to attend the film's premiere at the Cannes Film Festival.

Spicy and Racy

Paris has also continued to appear in the news by sparking scandals. She caused a stir in 2005 when she filmed a racy commercial for the fast-food chain Carl's Jr. In the advertisement, Paris washes a black

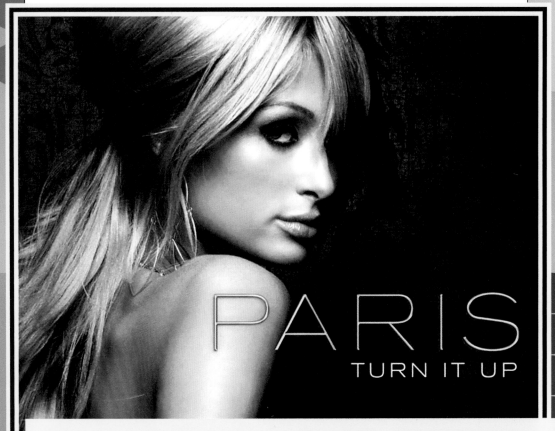

The cover for Paris Hilton's song "Turn it Up," which appeared on her 2006 debut album. The song hit number one on the Billboard US Hot Dance Club Play Chart. *Paris* received some favorable reviews; overall, music critics seemed pleasantly surprised with the album. It has sold nearly a million copies to date.

sports car while wearing nothing but high heels, diamonds, and a skimpy black bathing suit. She writhes on the car, covering herself with soapy water, all the time eating a giant Carl's Jr. hamburger.

Some critics, including a conservative media watchdog group called the Parents Television Council, felt the advertisement went too far. They called for Carl's Jr. to take the "sexually graphic" ad off the air. Of course, this controversy only made the ad more popular. It has been downloaded onto thousands of Web sites and has spawned numerous **parodies**. The CEO of Carl's Jr. told *USA Today* that the ad had generated more than $25 million in free media coverage.

Paris received more bad press in 2006 after an incident in which one of her boyfriends, Brandon Davis, made **vulgar** remarks to paparazzi about actress Lindsay Lohan while Paris laughed and egged him on. Later that year she struck up a friendship with pop star Britney Spears, but both were criticized after a series of embarrassing nightclub appearances together. AOL even named the pair Worst Celebrity Role Models of 2006.

In a more serious incident, Paris was arrested in September 2006 and charged with drunk driving. She told the officers that pulled her over that she had been speeding because she wanted to get a burger before the restaurant closed. Paris was fined about $1,500, her license was suspended, and she was placed on probation for 36 months. She was also ordered to attend an alcohol counseling program. When she was caught driving in March 2007 despite the fact that her license was suspended, the celebrity heiress faced the very real possibility that she might spend some time in prison.

Paris will probably recover from these mishaps, as she has in the past. She wrote in her book:

> **"I've learned you don't grow that much when things are good; you really grow in the tough times. When you get hurt, life gets very real, and then you have to stop and put the world in focus. . . . I know more than every how lucky I am, how blessed I've been."**

Both Paris and Nicky Hilton have been blessed with wealth, beauty, and a loving and supportive family. With all the power of their family name behind them and all of America at their feet, they can't help but do amazing things with their lives.

1981   **February 17** Paris Whitney Hilton is born in New York City.

1983   **October 5** Nicholai Olivia Hilton is born in New York City.

1985   Rick and Kathy Hilton move their family from New York to Bel-Air.

1996   The Hilton family moves back to New York. Paris enrolls at the Professional Children's School in Manhattan.

1997   The Hilton sisters attend Marissa Bregman's Sweet Sixteen party at the River Club in Manhattan where they first gain media attention as party girls. The term "celebutante" is coined to describe the Hilton sisters and their wealthy friends.

1998   Paris is enrolled in a program for troubled children in Utah.

1999   Paris mysteriously disappears from the Dwight School in Manhattan.

2000   Paris and Nicky are interviewed for a lead article in the September issue of *Vanity Fair* magazine, which also features photos of Paris.

2002   Nicky graduates from the Convent of the Sacred Heart high school and enters the Parsons School of Design.

Paris gets engaged to model Jason Shaw.

2003   **November** Video clips of Paris and Rick Salomon having sex are posted on the Internet.

December 3 *The Simple Life* premieres on Fox.

Paris ends her engagement with Jason Shaw and begins dating Backstreet Boy Nick Carter.

2004   Nicky launches a clothing line, Chick by Nicky Hilton.

Confessions of an Heiress, authored by Paris, is published.

Paris debuts her first perfume, "Paris Hilton."

The second season of *The Simple Life* airs.

August 14 Nicky marries Todd Meister in Las Vegas.

November The marriage between Nicky and Todd Meister is annulled.

2005 Nicky is banned forever from Los Angeles restaurant Il Sole for drunken behavior.

May *House of Wax* premieres.

Paris launches her second perfume, "Just Me."

The first Club Paris nightclub opens in Orlando; however, Nicky must fill in at the ribbon-cutting because Paris arrives six hours late.

Paris becomes engaged to Greek shipping heir Paris Latsis, but the engagement ends three months later.

The third season of *The Simple Life* airs on Fox.

2006 Nicky launches Nicky Hilton Beverly Hills clothing line.

January *National Lampoon's Pledge This!* is released on DVD.

Paris's single "Stars are Blind" is released, followed by her debut album, *Paris*.

September Paris is charged with driving under the influence of alcohol; her licence is suspended and she is sentenced to 36 months of probation.

2007 Paris releases the single "I Want You."

Club Paris owners end their association with the heiress, claiming that she had not fulfilled her obligations to attend events at the club.

June After being caught driving with a suspended license, Paris serves a 23-day prison sentence for violating her parole.

ACCOMPLISHMENTS & AWARDS

Albums (Paris)
2006   *Paris*

Singles (Paris)
2006   "Stars Are Blind"
           "Turn It Up"
           "Nothing in This World"

2007   "I Want You"

Films
2001   *Zoolander* (Paris)

2003   *The Cat in the Hat* (Paris)
           Wonderland (Paris)

2004   *Win a Date with Tad Hamilton!* (Paris)

2005   *House of Wax* (Paris)

2006   *National Lampoon's Pledge This!* (Paris and Nicky)

Books (Paris)
2004   *Confessions of an Heiress*
           The Tinkerbell Hilton Diaries: My Life Tailing Paris Hilton

2005   *Your Heiress Diary: Confess It All to Me*

Television (Paris)
2003   *The Simple Life* (Fox and E!)

2004   *The Simple Life* (Fox and E!)

2005   *The Simple Life* (Fox and E!)

2006   *The Simple Life* (Fox and E!)

2007   *The Simple Life* (Fox and E!)

Awards Won (Paris)
2005   Choice Movie Scream Scene, Teen Choice Awards

Books

Hilton, Paris. *Confessions of an Heiress.* New York: Simon & Schuster, 2004.

Mair, George. *Paris Hilton: The Naked Truth.* New York: Penguin, 2004.

Oppenheimer, Jerry. *House of Hilton.* New York: Crown Publishers, 2006.

Web Sites

http://houseofwaxmovie.warnerbros.com

The promotional site for Paris's movie *House of Wax* includes the movie trailer, video, and information about the upcoming DVD.

http://parishiltonrecord.com

This Web site focuses on Paris's music ventures and includes photos, videos, clips from her album, and a link to Paris's Myspace page.

www.myspace.com/parishilton

Paris's official Myspace page features Paris's daily blog, information about her music career, and an area for fans with photos and ways to contact Paris.

www.parishilton.com

Paris Hilton's official Web site includes a list of her public appearances, clips from her album and singles, and various news items related to Paris.

www.youtube.com/profile?user=ParisHilton

Paris's official YouTube channel gives fans a chance to view Paris's music videos.

amicable—done in a friendly way, without showing bad feelings.

annulment—a ruling that a marriage is invalid, and was never a true marriage.

audacity—boldness or daring.

boutique—a small specialty shop that sells fashionable merchandise

entourage—a group of attendants or associates who accompany an important person.

jaded—no longer interested in something, generally because it has been done too much.

kowtow—to act in a submissive way toward somebody with power or authority; to act like a servant or inferior.

notoriety—being known for some unfavorable quality or action.

parody—a piece of writing, music, film, or art that deliberately copies another work in a humorous way, or to make fun of the original work.

persona—a role or public image that is different from the person's private self.

pornographic—sexually explicit; intended to cause sexual arousal.

schadenfreude—satisfaction or pleasure at someone else's misfortune.

scion—a child or descendant of a famous, important, or wealthy family.

sequester—to withdraw into a private area.

sibling—a brother or sister.

tempestuous—turbulent, giving rise to many emotions.

vulgar—crude, indecent, or obscene.

page

2: Star Max Photos
6: Abaca Press/KRT
9: Fox TV/KRT
10: Star Max Photos
12: Walt Disney World/NMI
15: UPI Photo Archive
17: WENN Photos
18: Fashion Wire Daily Photos
20: Splash News
22: WENN Photos
24: Star Max Photos
27: Icon Images
28: Shane Gritzinger/Big Pictures US
29: Newswire Photos

31: Tim Aylen/Vision/PRN Photos
33: Fashion Wire Daily Photos
34: Billy Farrell/PMC/Sipa Press
36: Walt Disney World/NMI
39: AdMedia/Sipa Press
40: Nicolas Khayat/Abaca Press
43: Fox TV/KRT
44: Warner Bros. Pictures/NMI
47: FilmMagic
48: New Millennium Images
50: WireImage
53: UPI Newspictures
54: New Millennium Images

Front cover: Star Max Photos
Back cover: Walt Disney World/NMI

ABOUT THE AUTHOR

Emma Carlson Berne has written and edited over a dozen books for children and young adults, including biographies of Laura Ingalls Wilder, Christopher Columbus, and the rapper Snoop Dogg. She lives in Charleston, South Carolina.